ISHA UPANISHAD

ईशोपनषिद्

(Īśā Upaniṣad)

Elucidation by

Dr. T. R. Khanna

Published by:

Wisdom Publishers Organization, Inc.
WisdomPublsihers.org
info@sharelight.com

ISBN Paperback: 978-0-9727185-3-0
ISBN eBook: 978-0-9727185-4-7

Table of Contents

Preface v
IAST Transliteration Table. vii
Invocation 1
Mantra 1 4
Mantra 2 8
Mantra 3 11
Mantra 4 14
Mantra 5 18
Mantra 6 21
Mantra 7 24
Mantra 8 27
Mantra 9 31
Mantra 11 34
Mantra 11 37
Mantra 12 41
Mantra 13 45
Mantra 14 48
Mantra 15 52
Mantra 16 55
Mantra 17 58
Mantra 18 61
Gems of Wisdom 65

Preface

The Isha Upanishad is one of one hundred and eight Upanishads. It comes from the last chapter of the Yajurveda. Among Upanishads, it is one of the most important, because it teaches the fundamentals of consciousness. Isha comes from Ishavasya, the first word of the opening verse. 'Ishavasya' means pervaded by Consciousness, and 'Upanishad' means to receive wisdom of the soul at the feet of a Preceptor.

The Isha Upanishad teaches us that both metaphysical and analytical knowledge are necessary in life. They must be applied to life simultaneously if we are to live free from confusion and suffering. Action without understanding leads to blindness; knowledge detached from responsibility leads to deeper obscurity. Liberation arises through their integration.

The Isha Upanishad presents a complete and coherent vision of life, knowledge, and action. A central teaching is that **action and knowledge are not opposed**.

The initial verses make it clear that we are all the micro of the Macro. We are permeated with the same Essence that created and permeates the whole of creation. Later verses chide us to practice spiritual knowledge, and also to attain worldly knowledge. Lastly, we are reminded that this body will one day be reduced to ashes, and we must connect to our Absolute nature. Only then can we live without pain and conflict.

This edition of the Isha Upanishad includes the publisher's commentary on each mantra. After the conclusion of the Isha Upanishad, we have included 108 gems of wisdom drawn from the discourses of Dr. T. R. Khanna.

IAST Transliteration Table

Devanāgarī	IAST	English word sound
VOWELS		
अ	a	'u' in but / cup
आ	ā	'a' in father
इ	i	'i' in sit
ई	ī	'e' in seat
उ	u	'u' in put
ऊ	ū	'oo' in pool
ऋ	ṛ	'r' in curd / cricket
ॠ	ṝ	(long ṛ)
ए	e	'a' in save
ऐ	ai	'i' in pie
ओ	o	'o' in coat
औ	au	'ow' in cow
SEMIVOWELS		
य	ya	'ya' in yard
र	ra	'r' in rule
ल	la	'l' in leaf
व	va	'v' in vase
CONSONANTS		
ङ	ṅa	'ng' in king
च	ca	'c' in chap

छ	cha	‘ch’ in catcher
ज	ja	‘j’ in jog
झ	jha	‘ge’ in hedgehog
ञ	ña	‘ni’ in onion
ट	ṭa	‘t’ in stable
ठ	ṭha	‘th’ in ant-hill
ड	ḍa	‘da’ in dart
ढ	ḍha	‘dh’ in redhead
ण	ṇa	‘n’ in gentle
त	ta	‘t’ in tea
थ	tha	‘th’ in boathouse
द	da	‘d’ in desk
ध	dha	‘dh’ in adhere
न	na	‘n’ in nine
प	pa	‘p’ in pie
फ	pha	‘ph’ in uphold
ब	ba	‘b’ in butter
भ	bha	‘bh’ in abhor
म	ma	‘m’ in mutter
श	śa	‘sh’ in shawl
ष	ṣa	‘sh’ in push
स	sa	‘s’ in soul
ह	ha	‘h’ in hand
SPECIAL SIGNS		
◌ं	ṃ	‘m’ in yum (nasal)
◌ः	ḥ	(echo of breath)
◌्	—	vowel ‘a’ suppressor

Invocation
(Śānti Mantra)

ॐ पूर्णमदः पूर्णमिदं पूर्णात् पूर्णमुदच्यते ।
पूर्णस्य पूर्णमादाय पूर्णमेवावशिष्यते ॥
ॐ शान्तिः शान्तिः शान्तिः ॥

OṀ PŪRṆAM ADAḤ PŪRṆAM IDAṀ PŪRṆĀT
PŪRṆAM UDACYATE |
PŪRṆASYA PŪRṆAM ĀDĀYA PŪRṆAM
EVĀVAŚIṢYATE ||
OṀ ŚĀNTIḤ ŚĀNTIḤ ŚĀNTIḤ ||

Word-by-Word Meaning

- ॐ (OṀ) — the name/vibration of the Absolute, the Essence of All
- पूर्णम् (pūrṇam) — full, complete, whole, lacking nothing
- अदः (adaḥ) — That; the unmanifest, transcendent aspect of Reality; the Absolute
- पूर्णम् (pūrṇam) — full, complete
- इदम् (idam) — this; the manifest existence; life, Atman made manifest as the living self

- पूर्णात् (pūrṇāt) — from completeness (from fullness, perfection)
- पूर्णम् (pūrṇam) — fullness, completeness
- उदच्यते (udacyate) — arises, issues forth, is projected
- पूर्णस्य (pūrṇasya) — of the full, complete
- पूर्णम् (pūrṇam) — fullness, completeness
- आदाय (ādāya) — having taken, without loss
- पूर्णम् (pūrṇam) — fullness, completeness
- एव (eva) — indeed, surely, positively
- अवशिष्यते (avaśiṣyate) — remains
- शान्तिः (śānti) — peace

Translation

That (the Absolute, Supreme Self) is complete, full. This (Self, living self) is complete, full.

Fullness is permeated with fullness; the Self is pervaded by the Supreme Self. Fullness is manifested from Fullness and Fullness remains ever full.

Elucidation

The fullness of Consciousness permeates everything that is manifested: the sun, moon, stars, galaxies, and the space between them. The fullness of Consciousness also permeates this human incarnation.

We have all been born from that Fullness. Although the body

is finite, the soul is infinite. From the point of view of soul, we never die; we just change form according to our karma.

If we understand that we are projected from the fullness of eternity, we can never feel sorry for ourselves. We experience pain only when we forget our real state of fullness and identify, instead, with our persona.

Our persona is constantly projecting dreams and images based on its contact with the gross. When we chase these dreams, it creates a stir in the mind, and therefore, pain. No matter what we try to fill ourselves with: food, man, woman, children, or possessions, if we do not fill ourselves with the Supreme Fullness, we will remain empty.

If we remain established in Supreme Fullness, then we don't have to spend our lives chasing images. But to do that, we have to train our mind to enjoy our Supreme Fullness. We have to read inspiration daily, do good action daily, and become deeper every day. If we live life remembering our eternity, we can avoid a lot of worldly problems.

— *COMMENTARY* —

The invocation establishes **fullness, completeness** as the essence of Reality. Manifestation (life, existence) does not alter, change or diminish ultimate reality.

Mantra 1

ईशावास्यमिदं सर्वं यत्किञ्च जगत्यां जगत् ।
तेन त्यक्तेन भुञ्जीथा मा गृधः कस्यस्विद्धनम् ॥

ĪŚĀVĀSYAM IDAṀ SARVAṀ YAT KIÑCA
JAGATYĀṀ JAGAT |
TENA TYAKTENA BHUÑJĪTHĀ MĀ GṚDHAḤ
KASYASVID DHANAM ||

Word-by-Word Meaning

- ईशा (īśā) — Consciousness, the governing principle; that which regulates and orders
- आवास्यम् (āvāsyam) — to be dwelt in, pervaded, inhabited
- इदम् (idam) — this, what is immediately present
- सर्वम् (sarvam) — all, everything
- यत् (yat) — whatever
- किञ्च (kiñca) — even the smallest thing
- जगत्याम् (jagatyām) — in the world characterized by movement
- जगत् (jagat) — that which moves or changes
- तेन (tena) — by that understanding

- त्यक्तेन (tyaktena) — by relinquishing ownership or possessiveness
- भुञ्जीथा (bhuñjīthā) — enjoy, sustain oneself, live responsibly
- मा (mā) — do not
- गृधः (gṛdhaḥ) — crave, covet
- कस्य (kasya) — of anyone
- स्वित् (svit) — at all
- धनम् (dhanam) — possessions, wealth, means of enjoyment

Translation

All this—whatever moves within this moving world—is pervaded by Īśa, Supreme Consciousness. Therefore, live by relinquishing possessiveness; do not covet what belongs to others.

Elucidation

This body is the residence of Supreme Consciousness. Although it appears to be ours, in reality it is not ours. It is a very temporary residence for the soul. Similarly, the whole universe appears to be real, yet it, too, will be gone in a few million years.

This phenomenal world is always changing, and everything in it appears to be in motion. We are moved by gross phenomena unless we are full inside. If we remember that all gross manifestations are temporary, then we won't be moved by them.

In other words, we have to learn that anything we see with our eyes is temporary, and that only Supreme Consciousness is permanent. We should see everything as a moving drama, and not be upset by it. We have to go beyond phenomena, beyond the body, to understand creation from the point of view of consciousness.

The problem is that we want to experience Supreme Consciousness, but we also want to pursue worldly images. We cannot pursue both paths.

We should learn to enjoy the Supreme state of consciousness. To have good health, good principles, and to live in consciousness is our real wealth. How can worldly wealth be ours, when this body does not remain ours? If we understand the phenomenal world from this point of view, then we can renounce all feelings of jealousy and greed. We will not covet anyone's property or seek anyone's inheritance.

We say that this is my son, my daughter, my property. In fact, these relationships are just fleeting instances of this incarnation. To consider them permanent causes bondage, and bondage causes pain. It doesn't mean that we should be callous or negligent in our duty. Rather, we should understand that all relations and all possessions are part of this incarnation only. After this life is over, there is again Supreme Consciousness.

To understand life from the point of view of eternity, we need to free ourselves from all self-centered activity of the mind, and from all selfish motives. We have to leave behind our lethargic states of wanting what others have. We have to work on ourselves.

— *COMMENTARY* —

The opening mantra of the Isha Upanishad establishes the all-pervasive nature of Consciousness as the fundamental principle of existence. The world is not to be rejected. We must live in this world without possessiveness. This understanding avoids both materialism and escapist renunciation.

Mantra 2

कुर्वन्नेवेह कर्माणि जिजीविषेच्छतं समाः ।
एवं त्वयि नान्यथेतोऽस्ति न कर्म लिप्यते नरे ॥

KURVANN EVEHA KARMĀṆI JIJĪVIṢECCHATAṀ SAMĀḤ |
EVAṀ TVAYI NĀNYATHETO'STI NA KARMA LIPYATE NARE ||

Word-by-Word Meaning

- कुर्वन् (kurvan) — while doing, while acting
- एव (eva) — alone, indeed
- इह (iha) — here, in this world
- कर्माणि (karmāṇi) — actions, works, duties
- जिजीविषेत् (jijīviṣet) — should wish to live
- शतम् (śatam) — a hundred
- समाः (samāḥ) — years
- एवम् (evam) — in this manner
- त्वयि (tvayi) — for you
- न (na) — not
- अन्यथा (anyathā) — otherwise
- इतः (itaḥ) — from this

- अस्ति (asti) — there is
- न कर्म (na karma) — no action
- लिप्यते (lipyate) — clings, adheres, binds
- नरे (nare) — to a person, to a human being

Translation

By performing actions, work and meditation in this life, one should desire to live for one hundred years. In this way, oh man (oh living being), actions do not produce attachment. There is no other way.

Elucidation

To understand consciousness, we need to do our duty, free from attachment. In these hundred years of life, we should perfect our nature by doing action, rather than getting attached to the results of our actions.

Attachment to the body and its actions is the cause of pain. For example, a lot of people do body building so that they can have a muscular looking body. If something were to happen to their beautiful body, their whole life would be destroyed.

We have to keep the body fit, but we cannot become attached to its form. We should use the body for service, for good work, and to learn to live in consciousness. Then, whether we are young, old, or have an imperfect body, we can live happily.

We cannot live happily by getting attached only to things we like to do. The mind always wants something exciting, but excitement does not produce stability. When stability is missing, we become frustrated. In frustration, lies pain.

If we are to enjoy the full span of this incarnation, we have to perfect our nature through wisdom, satsang, meditation, and doing good action. We have to gain knowledge of our Supreme nature.

— *COMMENTARY* —

Action is unavoidable. When performed without possessiveness, it does not bind. This directly clarifies Mantra 1 and prevents the error of egoistic inaction (false renunciation).

Responsibly performing actions in this life, we should simply wish to live a full life span without getting excited or depressed. Living like this (without ego and attachment), actions do not cause bondage.

Mantra 3

असूर्या नाम ते लोका अन्धेन तमसावृताः ।
ताँस्ते प्रेत्याभिगच्छन्ति ये के चात्महनो जनाः ॥

ASURYĀ NĀMA TE LOKĀ ANDHENA
TAMASĀVṚTĀḤ |
TĀṀSTE PRETYĀBHIGACCHANTI YE KE
CĀTMAHANO JANĀḤ ||

Word-by-Word Meaning

- असूर्याः (asuryāḥ) — without illumination or light
- नाम (nāma) — named, designated, called
- ते (te) — those
- लोकाः (lokāḥ) — worlds, states of experience
- अन्धेन (andhena) — by blindness
- तमसा (tamasā) — darkness, ignorance
- आवृताः (āvṛtāḥ) — covered, enveloped
- तान् (tān) — those
- ते (te) — indeed
- प्रेत्य (pretya) — after death, after departing
- अभिगच्छन्ति (abhigacchanti) — go toward, enter
- ये (ye) — who

- के च (ke ca) — whoever
- आत्महनः (ātma-hanaḥ) — destroyers or negators of the self
- जनाः (janāḥ) — persons, people

Translation

Those who are engrossed in blinding darkness remain in a dying state. They are enveloped in ignorance. They are murdering their own soul.

Elucidation

People whose minds are negative are shrouded in darkness. They are murdering their own soul. They are depressed, and they make those around them miserable.

When people get involved with negative states of mind, they hurt themselves and others. They are easily excited and depressed because they have forgotten their original state, their essence, their fullness. Those who are slaying their soul in this incarnation will not have a good next incarnation, either. Hence, it is everyone's duty to break the cycle of negativity and evolve to a higher state of consciousness. Only then can the shrouds of darkness be removed from the mind.

When we are very attached to our name and form, we cannot experience the vital force. That's when our problems begin. But when we train our mind and senses to be in the subtlest state, we transcend gross difficulties. They still may arise, but we are able to deal with them without losing peace of mind.

When we establish ourselves in Supreme Consciousness, we will have a disciplined and happy life. Discipline means that we will not go crazy with negative feelings and emotions. They will exist as waves upon the surface of the ocean, but we will remain in the ocean's depth.

— *COMMENTARY* —

This mantra describes the consequence of denying one's true nature. Ignoring the truth and holding onto our ego and images is the equivalent of committing a slow suicide. We were not born to suffer and die—we were born to thrive and manifest our true Self.

Mantra 4

अनेजदेकं मनसो जवीयो
नैनद्देवा आप्नुवन्पूर्वमर्षत् ।
तद्धावतोऽन्यानत्येति तिष्ठत्
तस्मिन्नपो मातरिश्वा दधाति ॥

ANEJAD EKAM MANASO JAVĪYO
NAINAD DEVĀ ĀPNUVAN PŪRVAM ARṢAT |
TAD DHĀVATO'NYĀN ATYETĪ TIṢṬHAT
TASMINN APO MĀTARIŚVĀ DADHĀTI ||

Word-by-Word Meaning

- अनेजत् (aneját) — not moving, unmoving, changeless
- एकम् (ekam) — one, without a second
- मनसः (manasaḥ) — of the mind
- जवीयः (javīyaḥ) — swifter, faster
- न (na) — not
- एनत् (enat) — this (principle)
- देवाः (devāḥ) — faculties, luminous powers of perception
- आप्नुवन् (āpnuvan) — reach, attain
- पूर्वम् (pūrvam) — beforehand, prior

- अर्षत् (arṣat) — it goes ahead, precedes
- तत् (tat) — that
- धावतः (dhāvataḥ) — of those running
- अन्यान् (anyān) — others
- अत्येति (atyeti) — surpasses, goes beyond
- तिष्ठत् (tiṣṭhat) — standing still
- तस्मिन् (tasmin) — in that
- अपः (apaḥ) — energies, vital currents
- मातरिश्वा (mātariśvā) — life-force, prāṇa
- दधाति (dadhāti) — places, establishes, sustains

Translation

The Changeless, permanent Self, Atman, is One Without a Second. This Consciousness is faster than the mind and senses. It is the force behind these faculties. Standing still (changeless and all-pervading), It surpasses the running mind and senses. This life force (Prana) energizes every particle of existence.

Elucidation

Atman, Consciousness, is One Without a Second, permanent, changeless. Its activity is present in all living and non-living things. Consciousness is motionless, yet it transcends everything that is moving because it is omniscient. Omniscient, Omnipresent Reality is Consciousness.

Consciousness is faster than the mind, and more subtle than the senses. It is the force behind our living existence. It is the life force within the living body; it causes the mind and senses to perceive, yet it cannot be perceived by the gross mind or senses.

The senses want to perceive Consciousness, yet they are unable to do it. The eyes want to see it, yet they cannot see it. The ears want to hear it, yet they cannot hear it. The nose wants to smell Consciousness, but it cannot smell it. Consciousness cannot be tasted by the tongue. It cannot be touched by the hands. The organs of perception are incompetent to perceive Consciousness unless the mind is tuned to the subtlest state.

To experience Consciousness, we have to train our mind and senses to be in the subtlest state. As we have to train our mind and ears to appreciate classical music, similarly, we have to train our listening, our perception, and our touch to experience the Supreme. If, however, our mind and senses are constantly preoccupied with maintaining the material world, then Consciousness will elude us.

Our problem is that we do not train ourselves to experience the Supreme Nature. Instead, we train ourselves to experience our gross mind and feelings. We have to set aside our mental states and train our mind to experience the subtlest state. That subtle state exists in every molecule in the form of prana, the subtle force. Through it, Consciousness controls all the manifestations of the universe.

Prana sustains the whole universe, and it is also present in each one of us. Prana is in all forms of gross existence, in matter, and in all that is manifested in the ether. It is prana, the vital force, which is making us perceive. We hear because of prana. Our eyes shine because of prana. Prana is everywhere. All we have to do is remember it.

When we are very attached to our name and form, we cannot experience the vital force. That's when our problems begin. But when we train our mind and senses to be in the subtlest state, we transcend gross difficulties. They still may arise, but we are able to deal with them without losing peace of mind.

When we establish ourselves in Supreme Consciousness, we will have a disciplined and happy life. Discipline means that we will not go crazy with negative feelings and emotions. They will exist as waves upon the surface of the ocean, but we will remain in the ocean's depth.

— *COMMENTARY* —

This mantra describes the Self as motionless yet moving faster than the senses. It is beyond sensory and mental reach. Consciousness is the essence that makes motion, perception, and vitality possible.

Mantra 5

तदेजति तन्नैजति
तद्दूरे तद्वन्तिके ।
तदन्तरस्य सर्वस्य
तदु सर्वस्यास्य बाह्यतः ॥

TAD EJATI TANNAIJATI
TAD DŪRE TAD VANTIKE |
TAD ANTARASYA SARVASYA
TAD U SARVASYĀSYA BĀHYATAḤ ||

Word-by-Word Meaning

- तत् (tat) — that, ultimate reality
- एजति (ejati) — moves
- न एजति (na ejati) — does not move
- दूरे (dūre) — far
- अन्तिके (antike) — near
- अन्तरस्य (antarasya) — within
- सर्वस्य (sarvasya) — of all
- उ (u) — indeed
- बाह्यतः (bāhyataḥ) — outside, beyond

Translation

That (the Self) moves; it does not move.
It is far; it is near.
It is within all of this.
It is outside all of this.

Elucidation

Consciousness is all-permeating. Because it is all-permeating, so it permeates our perception, our thinking, the functioning of our senses. It permeates our actions and interactions; it permeates everything on this physical plane.

If we are established in that Supreme Consciousness, then we have practically no pain in life. When we are established in that state, we no longer seek the praise of uncentered people, nor are we upset by their blame. Praise and blame come only when we are in our ego.

Ego arises from ignorance, and ignorant people are incapable of attaining that state of Supreme Consciousness. Hence, egotistic people are far away from their Supreme Consciousness. They live in their own little space, like a frog in a well.

Through negative feelings, thought patterns, and actions, we suppress our soul. When we live in ego, the experience of Consciousness is far, far removed from us. Like the frog in the well who cannot experience being in the ocean, we also are unable to experience the ocean of Consciousness when we are trapped in our ego.

When we live in Supreme Consciousness, our soul is evolving. To continue evolving, we have to make fundamental changes in ourselves. That can only happen when we come in contact with the wise and stay in their company.

— *COMMENTARY* —

The Self is not an object limited by time and space or physical dimensions. The Self permeates the entire universe from the smallest particle to the greatest galaxy. The Self is closer to us than our thought—even the mind cannot fully grasp the magnitude or subtility of Consciousness.

Mantra 6

यस्तु सर्वाणि भूतान्यात्मन्येवानुपश्यति
सर्वभूतेषु चात्मानं ततो न विजुगुप्सते ॥

YAS TU SARVĀṆI BHŪTĀNY
ĀTMANYEVĀNUPAŚYATI
SARVA-BHŪTEṢU CĀTMĀNAṀ TATO NA
VIJUGUPSATE ||

Word-by-Word Meaning

- यः (yaḥ) — whoever
- तु (tu) — indeed
- सर्वाणि (sarvāṇi) — all
- भूतानि (bhūtāni) — beings, existents
- आत्मनि (ātmani) — in the Self
- एव (eva) — indeed
- अनुपश्यति (anupaśyati) — steadily perceives, continuously sees
- सर्वभूतेषु (sarva-bhūteṣu) — in all beings
- च (ca) — and
- आत्मानम् (ātmānam) — the Self
- ततः (tataḥ) — from that

- न (na) — not
- विजुगुप्सते (vijugupsate) — hates, feels aversion

Translation

One who perceives all beings in Consciousness (the Self), and Consciousness in all beings, does not hate.

Elucidation

All-Powerful Consciousness is perceived when we see everything from the point of view of eternity. We see Supreme Consciousness in others, without getting emotionally involved with their physical form. Hence, we are able to live beyond likes and dislikes, love and hatred.

The idea of revenge or hatred comes from ego. When we are established in Supreme Consciousness, we live beyond ego. Thus, we are also beyond love and hate; we are established in Supreme compassion.

Supreme compassion automatically comes when we are established in Supreme Consciousness. To be established, we have to make an effort not to be caught up with our body, not to be caught up with our mind, not to be caught up with our ego.

— *COMMENTARY* —

The perception of the oneness of Consciousness dissolves hatred and distain. The essence of every living being is Pure Consciousness. True love and compassion arise from the wisdom of Consciousness, not from manmade religion, images or dogma.

Mantra 7

यस्मिन्सर्वाणि भूतान्यात्मैवाभूद्विजानतः ।
तत्र को मोहः कः शोक एकत्वमनुपश्यतः ॥

YASMIN SARVĀṆI BHŪTĀNYĀTMAIVĀBHŪD VIJĀNATAḤ |
TATRA KO MOHAḤ KAḤ ŚOKA EKATVAM ANUPAŚYATAḤ ||

Word-by-Word Meaning

- यस्मिन् (yasmin) — in whom, for whom
- सर्वाणि (sarvāṇi) — all
- भूतानि (bhūtāni) — beings
- आत्मा (ātmā) — the Self
- एव (eva) — alone, indeed
- अभूत् (abhūt) — has become, is realized as
- विजानतः (vijānataḥ) — of the one who truly knows
- तत्र (tatra) — there, in that state
- कः (kaḥ) — what
- मोहः (mohaḥ) — delusion, confusion
- कः (kaḥ) — what
- शोकः (śokaḥ) — sorrow, grief

- एकत्वम् (ekatvam) — unity, oneness
- अनुपश्यतः (anupaśyataḥ) — of one who steadily perceives

Translation

For the one who knows Consciousess as all-pervading and sees the Immortal Self in everyone, what delusion and what sorrow can there be? Perceiving the unity and oneness of all existence, one has no false attachment.

Elucidation

What kind of delusion, what kind of sorrow will there be for the wise man who sees unity of existence, and perceives all beings as his own true self? Neither is he in conflict with himself, nor is he in conflict with others. He knows that conflict is born out of ego.

You see, fighting goes on within us, with our own ego. When we are under the influence of ego, we reject our own true self. We create inner conflict, and we create conflict with others. Pain only begins when we are hurting our own Supreme Nature. When we see ourselves and our relationships with others from the oneness of Supreme Consciousness, then our pain ends.

We have to look at ourselves and others as souls. From that point of view, we should go through life. All these friends and relatives we know have come to pay karmic debts, and we have come to pay our debts to them. To live in Supreme Consciousness means to remember, in all our actions, that we have come from the oneness of creation, and we all have to go back at the end of our journey. When we constantly imbibe the quality of Supreme Consciousness within us, we attain happiness that no one can take away.

— *COMMENTARY* —

Emotional suffering arises from ego and misperception, not from reality itself. When we live in soul awareness and see the same soul in everyone, sorrow and delusion dissolve. When we see everything from the point of view of Supreme Consciousness, our pain and suffering end.

Mantra 8

स पर्यगाच्छुक्रमकायमव्रणमस्नाविरं
शुद्धमपापविद्धम् ।
कविर्मनीषी परिभूः स्वयंभूर्याथातथ्यतोऽर्थान् व्यदधाच्छाश्वतीभ्यः
समाभ्यः ॥

SA PARYAGĀCCHUKRAM AKĀYAM AVRAṆAM
ASNĀVIRAM ŚUDDHAM APĀPA-VIDDHAM |
KAVIR MANĪṢĪ PARIBHŪḤ SVAYAMBHŪR
YĀTHĀTATHYATO’RTHĀN
VYADADHĀCCHĀŚVATĪBHYAḤ SAMĀBHYAḤ ||

Word-by-Word Meaning

- सः (saḥ) — that
- पर्यगात् (paryagāt) — has pervaded
- शुक्रम् (śukram) — luminous, radiant
- अकायम् (akāyam) — without body
- अव्रणम् (avraṇam) — without wound or defect
- अस्नाविरम् (asnāviram) — without sinews, without physical limitation
- शुद्धम् (śuddham) — pure

- अपापविद्धम् (apāpa-viddham) — untouched by evil or sins
- कविः (kaviḥ) — seer, one of direct insight
- मनीषी (manīṣī) — discerning, intelligent
- परिभूः (paribhūḥ) — all-surpassing, transcending all
- स्वयंभूः (svayambhūḥ) — self-existent
- याथातथ्यतः (yāthātathyataḥ) — exactly as they are, truly
- अर्थान् (arthān) — realities, purposes, meanings
- व्यदधात् (vyadadhāt) — has arranged, ordered
- शाश्वतीभ्यः (śāśvatībhyaḥ) — eternal
- समाभ्यः (samābhyaḥ) — harmonized principles, laws of equilibrium

Translation

Pure Consciousness pervades all. It is self-effulgent light, bodiless, invulnerable, devoid of any kind of superimposition which man creates. It is untouched by evil or sins. Our True Nature is all-seeing and all-knowing. It is all-pervading intelligence. Consciousness is self-manifest. The properties and characteristics of everything in this Universe are assigned in the proper way according to the inherent laws of Consciousness and nature.

Elucidation

The self-effulgent light of Supreme Consciousness is present in all of us. It is the Supreme light which enables the eyes to see. The same Supreme light brings us joy and makes us invulnerable to all vagaries of mind.

When we are in Supreme Consciousness, we are invulnerable. The moment we live in our body, we are vulnerable. Then we have stomach problems, headaches, all kinds of pains and worries.

Intellect cannot give understanding of Supreme Consciousness. Supreme Consciousness has to be perceived, and to perceive it, we have to devote time. We should spend twenty to thirty minutes daily in meditation and give the mind a chance to rest from thinking. When we stay in Supreme Consciousness, we are able to see our own, and other people's behavior clearly. We attain the quality of consciousness which is devoid of all mental superimpositions.

From the point of view of consciousness, we do not see that she is pretty or ugly, or he is handsome. We are not impressed by pompousness. We see the nature of people's behavior and are no longer attracted by their deceptive faces. We are not distracted by identification with our own male or female form.

Consciousness is sitting inside of us in its all-knowing state. It is reminding us that, although we have a certain form and attributes, our real duty is to gain insight into our eternal nature. Our duty is to bring light to all those with whom we come in contact, and tell them that we are not just body, mind, or ego. We are beyond all these things, and we are none of these things. We are permeated with the eternal light of Supreme.

We have to become established in eternity and do all duties in conformity with natural laws. We don't have to become caught in the narrowness of man-made images or dogmas, because these create conflict. Images are born out of ego and intellect. Consciousness gives rise to clear perception, pure intelligence, and inner glow that cannot be taken away.

— *COMMENTARY* —

This mantra gives the most precise and descriptive definition of the Self. It defines the nature of Consciousness without any symbolism, emotional sentiment or intellectual fancy. Pure Consciousness is beyond all material projections and limitations.

Mantra 9

अन्धं तमः प्रविशन्ति येऽविद्यामुपासते ।
ततो भूय इव ते तमो य उ विद्यायां रताः ॥

ANDHAṀ TAMAḤ PRAVIŚANTI YE'VIDYĀM UPĀSATE |
TATO BHŪYA IVA TE TAMO YA U VIDYĀYĀṀ RATĀḤ ||

Word-by-Word Meaning

- अन्धम् (andham) — blind
- तमः (tamaḥ) — darkness, ignorance
- प्रविशन्ति (praviśanti) — enter into
- ये (ye) — those who
- अविद्याम् (avidyām) — knowledge of analytical and physical sciences only
- उपासते (upāsate) — are devoted to, cling to
- ततः (tataḥ) — from that
- भूयः (bhūyaḥ) — greater, deeper
- इव (iva) — as it were
- ते (te) — those
- तमः (tamaḥ) — darkness

- ये (ye) — who
- उ (u) — indeed
- विद्यायाम् (vidyāyām) — Self-knowledge
- रताः (ratāḥ) — absorbed, delighted

Translation

Into blinding darkness enter those only devoted to knowledge of analytical and physical sciences. Into even greater darkness enter those devoted to Self-knowledge alone.

Elucidation

Into blinding darkness enter those who are absorbed only with analysis and discovery of the physical world. They are absorbed in action but lack wisdom of the Self.

Those who are devoted exclusively to the pursuit of Self-knowledge but do not practice, enter into even greater darkness. They don't get up early in the morning and purify their soul through meditation and study of scriptures. They do not apply wisdom to every aspect of their lives. They are philosophizing, but they are not practicing.

Hence, science without metaphysics is worthless, and metaphysics without practice is even worse.

— *COMMENTARY* —

Dedication to intellectual knowledge exclusive of spiritual knowledge (Wisdom) cannot remove ignorance. However, dedication to spiritual knowledge alone without action and understanding leads to even greater ignorance.

Mantra 10

अन्यदेवाहुर्विद्यया
अन्यदाहुरविद्यया ।
इति शुश्रुम धीराणां
ये नस्तद्विचचक्षिरे ॥

ANYAD EVĀHUR VIDYAYĀ
ANYAD ĀHUR AVIDYAYĀ |
ITI ŚUŚRUMA DHĪRĀṆĀṀ
YE NAS TAD VICACAKṢIRE ||

Word-by-Word Meaning

- अन्यत् (anyat) — different, distinct
- एव (eva) — indeed
- आहुः (āhuḥ) — they say, they declare
- विद्यया (vidyayā) — by Self-knowledge
- अन्यत् (anyat) — another, distinct
- आहुः (āhuḥ) — they say
- अविद्यया (avidyayā) — by worldly knowledge, by action without understanding
- इति (iti) — thus
- शुश्रुम (śuśruma) — we have heard

- धीराणाम् (dhīrāṇām) — of the wise, the discerning
- ये (ye) — who
- नः (naḥ) — to us
- तत् (tat) — that
- विचचक्षिरे (vicacakṣire) — clearly explained, made distinct

Translation

The wise say that the result of spiritual knowledge is indeed distinct from the result of worldly knowledge alone. Thus, we have heard from the Wise, who have clearly explained this to us.

Elucidation

Self-knowledge is attained differently than is worldly knowledge, and each has a distinct result. Worldly knowledge leads to analysis of nature and matter. Metaphysical analysis leads to soul analysis. Through it one asks questions such as, "What is my soul? Where do I come from? What is the real core of my being?"

The patient and wise men have explained that the result of doing nominal metaphysical analysis leads to only superficial understanding of the Self. By itself, it is not enough, just as worldly knowledge is also incomplete.

Physicists, after studying thirty or forty years, realize that they have attained intellectual understanding, but have not experienced Creation. Analytical study and practice of metaphysics have to proceed side by side. If we know physics, and also practice metaphysics: study scriptures, meditate, live a total life of spirituality, then we arrive at a very high state.

We need knowledge of both phenomena and noumena. One without the other is not sufficient. We cannot ignore worldly knowledge, because the body is dependent upon this phenomenal world. We have to know how to heat homes, how to grow food, how the sun affects certain herbs and spices.

But as important as physical knowledge is, we cannot forget that true happiness is dependent upon knowledge of the soul. A healthy body is not enough; a happy soul is also very important.

A happy soul is attained by practicing the Supreme knowledge of Supreme Consciousness.

Once we realize that both metaphysical and physical knowledge merge and submerge in each other, we arrive at the apex of our consciousness. We understand the phenomenal world, but we practice our spiritual practices and live in an ecstatic state.

— *COMMENTARY* —

Spiritual knowledge and worldly knowledge produce different results, and one without the other is incomplete. The authority of this teaching is grounded in the Vedas and in the wisdom of the Wise.

Mantra 11

विद्यां चाविद्यां च
यस्तद्वेदोभयं सह ।
अविद्यया मृत्युं तीर्त्वा
विद्ययाऽमृतमश्नुते ॥

VIDYĀṀ CĀVIDYĀṀ CA
YAS TAD VEDOBHAYAM SAHA |
AVIDYAYĀ MṚTYUṀ TĪRTVĀ
VIDYAYĀ'MṚTAM AŚNUTE ||

Word-by-Word Meaning

- विद्याम् (vidyām) — metaphysical knowledge, knowledge of Consciousness
- च (ca) — and
- अविद्याम् (avidyām) — worldly knowledge; knowledge of physical sciences
- च (ca) — and
- यः (yaḥ) — whoever
- तत् (tat) — that
- वेद (veda) — knows
- उभयम् (ubhayam) — both

- सह (saha) — together
- अविद्यया (avidyayā) — by physical knowledge
- मृत्युम् (mṛtyum) — death, limitation
- तीर्त्वा (tīrtvā) — having crossed over
- विद्यया (vidyayā) — by wisdom (soul-knowledge)
- अमृतम् (amṛtam) — the deathless
- अश्नुते (aśnute) — attains, realizes

Translation

Those who know and understand both physical and metaphysical sciences together achieve the results of both. By knowing physical science, we overcome death (the mental and physical maladies that lead to death). By knowing metaphysical science, we obtain eternal life (deathlessness).

Elucidation

Those who understand both metaphysical and physical sciences remove their ignorance and overcome the decay and death of this life. No sorrow touches them because they understand the real meaning of this incarnation.

We have to be worldly wise. We have to understand human nature; we have to know the laws of the land and how the world operates. We have to earn a living to sustain the body. But to get caught in seeking satisfaction from material things — cars, TV's, big homes — brings us close to bondage, decay and death. These things do not bring permanent happiness.

What gives permanent happiness is the cognitive study of the soul: sitting in meditation, trying to understand our real nature by studying the Upanishads and other scriptures. When we attain the knowledge of this eternal life in us, then we are free from the bondage of this worldly existence, although we partake of it to sustain the body.

It is fine to perfect the body, to perfect our environment, to perfect our homes, but we have to also attain samadhi, that ecstatic state. We need to be simultaneously worldly wise and established in the transcendental state. That is called samyama.

Spiritual life is not the antithesis to being worldly wise. In other words, contemplative life and active life should function simultaneously. Spiritual life without work results in the body being neglected. Similarly, having a muscle-bound body, but nothing of Absolute Consciousness in our mind, makes us nothing but robots of flesh. Neither should we be robots of flesh, nor should we be meditating, decaying flesh.

Knowledge of this empirical world must be transformed into the transcendental state — the highest spiritual experience of our existence. This universe exists for that Supreme Consciousness in us. We do not exist for the phenomenal world. The phenomenal world exists for us to realize that we are the micro of the Macro. For that, knowledge of both the manifest and the unmanifest are important.

— *COMMENTARY* —

Worldly knowledge and soul-knowledge practiced together make our life meaningful and fulfilling. Liberation arises from the integration of both worldly knowledge and spiritual wisdom.

Mantra 12

अन्धं तमः प्रविशन्ति
येऽसम्भूतिमुपासते ।
ततो भूय इव ते तमो
य उ सम्भूत्यां रताः ॥

ANDHAṀ TAMAḤ PRAVIŚANTI
YE' ASAMBHŪTIM UPĀSATE |
TATO BHŪYA IVA TE TAMO
YA U SAMBHŪTYĀṀ RATĀḤ ||

Word-by-Word Meaning

- अन्धम् (andham) — blind
- तमः (tamaḥ) — darkness, ignorance
- प्रविशन्ति (praviśanti) — enter into
- ये (ye) — those who
- असम्भूतिम् (asambhūtim) — the phenomenal world
- उपासते (upāsate) — are devoted to, worship
- ततः (tataḥ) — from that
- भूयः (bhūyaḥ) — greater
- इव (iva) — as it were
- ते (te) — those

- तमः (tamaḥ) — darkness
- ये (ye) — who
- उ (u) — indeed
- सम्भूत्याम् (sambhūtyām) — noumenon, the unmanifested
- रताः (ratāḥ) — absorbed, delighted

Translation

Into blinding darkness enter those devoted only to the phenomenal world; into even greater darkness, as it were, enter those devoted to noumenon alone.

Elucidation

Those who worship the phenomenal world enter into blinding darkness, and those who delight in the noumenon only, but do not apply the knowledge of consciousness to daily life, enter into even greater darkness.

When we are interested in phenomena only, we get caught up in the gross. We enjoy the beauty of a woman or a man, forgetting that everyone becomes wrinkled one day. We forget that everything of this world is going to end, and we cannot get attached to the phenomenal world in this way.

If we are caught up exclusively with the intellectual pursuit of spirituality, we will neglect our body, health, and environment. If we work, work, work, and neglect our soul, we will always be unhappy. We go wrong when we are taking care of only one aspect of our life.

These eyes see; these ears listen; this mouth speaks because of the breath of life. This universe is in motion because of prana, the breath of life. If we realize that there is a greater force than just the eyes, the ears, and the mouth, then we will realize our transcendental state.

There is something greater than the sun, the moon, and the stars. Beyond the nebulae, beyond the galaxies, there is something else. Beyond the manifest and beyond the unmanifest; the Essence of the universe is in existence. To experience that Essence is our transcendental state. That state is attained through meditation, meditative awareness, through study of the scriptures, through satsang, and through Self-realization.

The real majesty is to remain in a transcendental state — to work in the world, but not be caught up in it; to have relationships, but to be able to see everyone as souls who have come according to their own karmas.

We have to operate in this phenomenal world because we have a body. But we also must go beyond this phenomenal world to experience the transcendental state in which ecstasy exists. Once we experience that, we will never be unhappy.

— *COMMENTARY* —

Exclusive attention to either the manifest world (phenomenon) or the unmanifest principle (noumenon) leads to error. Only an integrated and balanced approach will lead to true happiness and fulfillment.

Mantra 13

अन्यदेवाहुः सम्भवादन्यदाहुरसम्भवात् ।
इति शुश्रुम धीराणां
ये नस्तद्विचचक्षिरे ॥

ANYAD EVĀHUḤ SAMBHAVĀD
ANYAD ĀHUR ASAMBHAVĀT |
ITI ŚUŚRUMA DHĪRĀṆĀṀ
YE NAS TAD VICACAKṢIRE ||

Word-by-Word Meaning

- अन्यत् (anyat) — different, distinct
- एव (eva) — indeed
- आहुः (āhuḥ) — they say, they declare
- सम्भवात् (sambhavāt) — by the unmanifest, noumenon
- अन्यत् (anyat) — another, distinct
- आहुः (āhuḥ) — they say
- असम्भवात् (asambhavāt) — by the manifest, phenomenon
- इति (iti) — thus
- शुश्रुम (śuśruma) — we have heard

- धीराणाम् (dhīrāṇām) — from the wise, the discerning
- ये (ye) — who
- नः (naḥ) — to us
- तत् (tat) — that
- विचचक्षिरे (vicacakṣire) — clearly explained

Translation

One result, they say, comes from a study of phenomenon, the manifest world. Another result, they say, comes from understanding the unmanifest, noumenon. Thus, we have heard from the wise who have clearly explained this to us.

Elucidation

The wise people have explained to us through the scriptures that analysis of the phenomenal world is incomplete; we also have to experience the noumenon state. In other words, scientific discovery without knowledge of the soul is not enough. Knowledge of the beginning of creation cannot be attained just by doing scientific studies.

Contemplation of the noumenon state alone is also not enough. Phenomenon and noumenon are not separate and distinct. We cannot understand one without the other.

If we are only contemplating on our soul, then we will neglect our body and our environment, and we will not know how to operate in this world. On the other hand, if our point of view is only from the materialistic level, then we will not know how to attain the highest spiritual understanding.

We got this human body to experience our eternity: the Absolute Nature in us, Ultimate Reality. One day we will go back to our essence. This is why it is very important that we study this phenomenal world from the point of view of eternity. When we know the noumenon state, then we can live in the phenomenal world, and its pain will not affect us.

To sit in a "high contemplative state" while the environment falls apart, our health falls apart, and our tummy bulges is horrible. We cannot neglect the body in which the soul lives; neither can we live just for the sake of the body — having a muscular body, but a head full of emotional stress.

Without knowledge, we cannot function in the world of phenomena, and without wisdom of the soul, we cannot live peacefully. Both are important. Both are taken care of when we understand our essence and also understand how to operate in the world of phenomena.

— *COMMENTARY* —

The result of studying phenomena is different than the result of studying spiritual knowledge. We cannot be effective in this world without worldly knowledge, but we cannot find true happiness without spiritual knowledge. Worldly existence and spiritual life are not opposed and the knowledge of both must be integrated.

Mantra 14

सम्भूतिं च विनाशं च
यस्तद्वेदोभयं सह ।
विनाशेन मृत्युं तीर्त्वा
सम्भूत्याऽमृतमश्नुते ॥

SAMBHŪTIṀ CA VINĀŚAṀ CA
YASTAD VEDOBHAYAM SAHA |
VINĀŚENA MṚTYUṀ TĪRTVĀ
SAMBHŪTYĀ'MṚTAM AŚNUTE ||

Word-by-Word Meaning

- सम्भूतिम् (sambhūtim) — noumenon, the unmanifest which never decays
- च (ca) — and
- विनाशम् (vināśam) — ever-changing phenomenon
- च (ca) — and
- यः (yaḥ) — whoever
- तत् (tat) — that
- वेद (veda) — knows
- उभयम् (ubhayam) — both

- सह (saha) — together
- विनाशेन (vināśena) — by ever-changing phenomenon
- मृत्युम् (mṛtyum) — death, limitation
- तीर्त्वा (tīrtvā) — crosses over, overcomes
- सम्भूत्याः (sambhūtyāḥ) — by noumenon
- अमृतम् (amṛtam) — immortality, deathlessness
- अश्नुते (aśnute) — attains, realizes

Translation

Whoever knows noumenon and phenomenon together, by knowledge of phenomenon overcomes death, and by knowledge of noumenon attains immortality.

Elucidation

We take birth, attain adulthood, old age, and die. We transform into something else. The phenomenal world is ever-changing. We are living on this earth planet — a ball that is surrounded by water, moving through space. We call it our home. But this is just a temporary stopping station in our eternal journey. For example, we landed either in America, Japan, India, or Africa. These are facts of our phenomenal existence.

Noumenon is the eternal principle, our eternal nature, and it is eternal law. We come from eternity. We know we have a body, but do we know why it was given to us? Was it given just to have fun, or to get married, have children, and then die from disease? No. It was given to us to experience our eternity so that we could always be happy and balanced. That's the crux of the issue of this human incarnation. If we understand this, then we are ecstatic. But if we don't understand, then we are caught in emotional and physical pain.

We need to keep the body healthy so that it doesn't become a nuisance. We need a healthy mind so that it doesn't bother us with negative feelings and emotions. This is why we are studying the Isha Upanishad. We're not studying just to understand the words. We are studying so that we can perfect our nature to experience our eternity, our noumenon state.

When we are established in noumenon, our senses, our prana, and our health fine tune on that Supreme Consciousness. We overcome decay and death of this body.

The body is not supposed to die of sickness. The body is supposed to serve its purpose until we leave it to go to eternity. If the body is sick our whole life, it means we haven't fine tuned the body and mind to Supreme Consciousness.

Fine tuning is very important if we want to overcome constant preoccupation with the gross body, mind, and senses. If we understand the ever-changing phenomenal world and also our eternal nature, then we are free. When we fine tune our mind to noumena, we can attain our goal of eternal joy while living in this incarnation.

— *COMMENTARY* —

Understanding the nature of this world and applying common sense frees us from unnecessary pain and suffering. At the same time, engaging in the deep study and understanding of ultimate reality leads to the direct experience of Eternity and the highest freedom.

Mantra 15

हिरण्मयेन पात्रेण
सत्यस्यापिहितं मुखम् ।
तत्त्वं पूषन्नपावृणु
सत्यधर्माय दृष्टये ॥

HIRAṆMAYENA PĀTREṆA
SATYASYĀPIHITAṀ MUKHAM |
TAT TVAṀ PŪṢANN APĀVṚṆU
SATYADHARMĀYA DṚṢṬAYE ||

Word-by-Word Meaning

- हिरण्मयेन (hiraṇmayena) — golden, radiant, dazzling
- पात्रेण (pātreṇa) — by a disc, covering
- सत्यस्य (satyasya) — of truth, of reality
- अपिहितम् (apihitam) — concealed, covered
- मुखम् (mukham) — face
- तत् (tat) — that
- त्वम् (tvam) — you
- पूषन् (pūṣan) — nourisher, illuminator
- अपावृणु (apāvṛṇu) — uncover, remove

- सत्यधर्माय (satya-dharmāya) — the true nature or law of the universe
- दृष्टये (dṛṣṭaye) — for seeing, for direct vision

Translation

The face of Ultimate Truth is covered by a golden disc. O Pūṣan, Light of lights, remove that covering so that we may have the direct perception of Truth.

Elucidation

As the sun is covered with clouds, the disc of our shining light (our soul) is covered with attractions of this worldly, materialistic outlook. When we cover our face with a mask, the real face cannot be seen. Similarly, our real nature is being masked by our materialistic outlook and the attractions of this materialistic world.

The body exists so that we can perfect our nature; it does not exist for its own sake. The mind exists to experience knowledge of eternity; it does not exist so that we can cater to its feelings or fluctuations, its attractions or repulsions.

Pain comes from constantly applying materialistic pressures on ourselves. We are seeking pleasure through ownership; instead, we are owned by things. When we see the glitter of material objects as the source of real happiness, we don't recognize the soul which is shining inside of us. The real gem, the shining light of soul is burning in us.

So, in this verse we are asking, "Oh Pushan, Oh Light of my soul, burn these materialistic clouds that are covering me." By applying knowledge of the soul to our daily actions, our false perception is removed. Our life is sparkled.

— *COMMENTARY* —

Truth is hidden by the glitter and false attraction of appearances, powers, and attainments that dazzle the intellect. The Truth-seeker seeks for direct vision, beyond all coverings and images.

Mantra 16

पूषन्नेकर्षे यम सूर्य प्राजापत्य
व्यूह रश्मीन् समूह ।
तेजो यत्ते रूपं कल्याणतमं
तत्ते पश्यामि योऽसावसौ पुरुषः सोऽहमस्मि ॥

PŪṢANN EKARṢE YAMA SŪRYA PRĀJĀPATYA
VYŪHA RAŚMĪN SAMŪHA |
TEJO YAT TE RŪPAṀ KALYĀṆATAMAṀ
TAT TE PAŚYĀMI YO'SĀVASAU PURUṢAḤ
SO'HAMASMI ||

Word-by-Word Meaning

- पूषन् (pūṣan) — Light of lights, nourisher, sustainer, illuminator
- एकर्षे (ekarṣe) — Ultimate knower, sole ruler
- यम (yama) — Controller, regulator, restrainer
- सूर्य (sūrya) — Sun of suns, illuminator, source of light
- प्राजापत्य (prājāpatya) — Light of Wisdom
- व्यूह (vyūha) — spread forth
- रश्मीन् (raśmīn) — rays, beams of light
- समूह (samūha) — gather up

- तेजः (tejaḥ) — radiance, brilliance
- यत् (yat) — which
- ते (te) — your
- रूपम् (rūpam) — form, appearance
- कल्याणतमम् (kalyāṇatamam) — most auspicious, most beneficial
- तत् (tat) — that
- ते (te) — your
- पश्यामि (paśyāmi) — I see, I behold
- यः (yaḥ) — who
- असौ (asau) — that there
- पुरुषः (puruṣaḥ) — indwelling conscious being, the Self
- सः (saḥ) — that
- अहम् (aham) — I
- अस्मि (asmi) — am

Translation

O Pūṣan, Light of lights, Ultimate Knower, Sun of suns, the Light of Wisdom. Spread forth your rays of wisdom. Gather up your radiant light and reveal your auspicious form. That Self in the sun, that Self I am.

Elucidation

Oh Light of lights, Knower of ultimate wisdom, spread forth Your rays, so that we may behold Your radiant light inside of us. Remove our darkness and make us perceive our soul, our Self. Make us see the loveliest form of Purusha, the real Self.

When we look into the face of someone who is meditating, we can see that person's ecstatic state. When we perceive our real Self, we automatically become radiant. We experience our eternal energy that is also in the light of the sun.

What is going on in the sun? An unbelievable explosion of self-effulgent light — phenomenal energy of the Essence. Millions and millions of hydrogen bombs are exploding and exploding, giving light to us 93 million miles away! That light is in us, so how dare we be depressed or emotional about something of this phenomenal world? How do we dare? How do we dare?

We should not take ourselves so emotionally that we forget we are the micro of the Macro. We are vast like the space, and our actions should be dedicated to that Eternal Nature. Early in the morning, we should revive that same energy in us that is also exploding in the sun.

We are the lone traveler on an eternal journey, yet we are not alone. We are, in fact, a manifestation of Supreme Energy. The entire universe is a manifestation of the Supreme. The essence of everything is the Supreme.

— COMMENTARY —

The energy that powers the sun is also animating this human incarnation. The essence of that light is the Light of Consciousness. We are the Light of Supreme Consciousness.

Mantra 17

वायुरनिलममृतमथेदं भस्मान्तं शरीरम् ।
ॐ क्रतो स्मर कृतं स्मर क्रतो स्मर कृतं स्मर ॥

VĀYUR ANILAM AMṚTAM ATHEDAṀ
BHASMĀNTAṀ ŚARĪRAM |
OṀ KRATO SMARA KṚTAṀ SMARA KRATO SMARA
KṚTAṀ SMARA ||

Word-by-Word Meaning

- वायुः (vāyuḥ) — the life force, vital breath
- अनिलम् (anilam) — cosmic breath, Cosmic Life Energy
- अमृतम् (amṛtam) — deathless, imperishable
- अथ (atha) — now, then
- इदम् (idam) — this
- भस्मान्तम् (bhasmāntam) — ending in ashes
- शरीरम् (śarīram) — body
- ॐ (oṁ) — totality, completeness, Essence of Being, Truth
- क्रतो (krato) — will, directing intelligence
- स्मर (smara) — remember
- कृतम् (kṛtam) — what has been done, actions performed

Translation

The life force returns to the Cosmic Life Force. Individual consciousness returns to Universal Consciousness. This body is reduced to ashes. Oh my mind, remember OM, remember the Essence. Remember the past deeds and karmas. Oh my mind, remember your deeds and remember the Ultimate Truth.

Elucidation

May our lives enter into Eternal Nature and Eternal Nature enter into our lives. May the individual life force be transformed into Cosmic Life Energy. May Cosmic Energy enter into our consciousness. Then may our soul enter into Cosmic Consciousness and remain hooked to it.

Oh my mind, remember the Supreme. Remember that this body is going to be finished. It's going to be reduced to ashes. Oh my mind, remember that this body is going to be reduced to ashes and remember what I need to do now to overcome the past deeds. Remember the past deeds and karmas so that I can go beyond this body.

Remember, oh my mind, why this human birth was given. Oh my mind, remember the Supreme.

— COMMENTARY —

In the final analysis, the body is reduced to ashes. Everything that is temporary is dissolved. When the mind-ego connection is broken, individuality and self-centeredness are dissolved and all that remains is OM, the Essence of Being.

The mind-ego connection is broken only when we remember that our own selfish desires and actions have created the conflict. What conflict? The conflict between what we think we are (separate individuals) and what we reallly are (Atman—Universal Consciousness).

Mantra 18

अग्ने नय सुपथा राये अस्मान्
विश्वानि देव वयुनानि विद्वान् ।
युयोध्यस्मज्जुहुराणमेनो
भूयिष्ठां ते नम उक्तिं विधेम ॥

AGNE NAYA SUPATHĀ RĀYE ASMĀN
VIŚVĀNI DEVA VAYUNĀNI VIDVĀN |
YUYODHYASMAJ JUHURĀṆAM ENO
BHŪYIṢṬHĀṀ TE NAMA UKTIṀ VIDHEMA ||

Word-by-Word Meaning

- अग्ने (agne) — Supreme Fire of fires; illuminating principle of determination
- नय (naya) — lead, guide
- सुपथा (supathā) — by the good path
- राये (rāye) — physical, mental, and spiritual prosperity; highest fulfillment
- अस्मान् (asmān) — us
- विश्वानि (viśvāni) — all
- देव (deva) — luminous, shining one
- वयुनानि (vayunāni) — ways, means, courses of action

- विद्वान् (vidvān) — knowing, discerning
- युयोधि (yuyodhi) — remove, drive away, destroy
- अस्मत् (asmat) — from us
- जुहुराणम् (juhurāṇam) — leading astray, crooked
- एनः (enaḥ) — error, wrongdoing
- भूयिष्ठाम् (bhūyiṣṭhām) — fullest, greatest
- ते (te) — to you
- नमउक्तिम् (nama-uktim) — expression of reverence, acknowledgment
- विधेम (vidhema) — we offer, we perform

Translation

O Agni, lead us by the virtuous path to the highest physical, mental and spiritual prosperity.

You know all our deeds and karmas. With your radiant divine qualities, destroy our self-deception and remove all the obstacles from our life. With our heartfelt offering (salutation) we are invoking your unfathomable grace.

Elucidation

Oh Fire of fires, lead us along the virtuous path. You know the whole universe of our past deeds, so please remove our obstacles: all deceitful and self-deceptive states of mind.

In other words, take away from us all the obstacles of self-deception such as, "Well, I'll do spiritual work when I get old," or "I'll know my true nature by attending a class." It's self-deception. Nobody ever evolves that way.

So, Ever-Shining Light, we ask You to lead us to physical, mental, and spiritual prosperity. We eternally offer to Thee our devotion and salutations.

— *COMMENTARY* —

The Upanishad closes not with withdrawal or denial but with acknowledgement, determination and affirmation.

We do not know the full extent of our past karmas or all their effects on our mind and body. Looking into our own soul, we seek the guidance of our Higher Nature to remove all the obstacles from our life. The greatest obstacles are our own ego and ignorance.

We acknowledge the work at hand—the purification of the mind—the need to remove our self-deception, bad habits and self-centeredness.

With this mantra we are invoking the power of Consciousness and the blessings of the Wise. The power inherent in Divine Wisdom is so great that it can obliterate everything that is unreal.

We assert and affirm our determination to continue our spiritual journey to the very end—to Eternity. In the end, we realize the Truth and we are free.

OM TAT SAT

Gems of Wisdom

From the discourses of Dr. T. R. Khanna

We sustain inspiration by always doing good work and keeping our attitude positive.

We can keep our body healthy by eating good food and exercising daily. We can keep our mind healthy by inspiring ourselves each day.

To realize our potential, we must apply ourselves.

To face difficulty with confidence is success. To be afraid of difficulty is failure.

True freedom is when we have total control over our thought patterns.

Each day is a new incarnation. Start it fresh!

Happiness doesn't just come. We have to work for it.

The best part of our life is the good that we do.

Sickness can come to anyone, but with
a healthy attitude we can heal.

We can be youthful at any age if we are positive,
inspiring ourselves, and making the best of now.

Make the best of every moment that life presents you.

The more energy you put into inspiration and
good actions, the happier you will be.

How do we remain youthful, even at a ripe old
age? By being energetic and positive, and keeping
the joy of noble thoughts in our heart.

Wisdom sharpens our minds and intelligence. It
makes us an asset to ourselves and others.

Self-improvement takes effort and practice.
It's a process that we should never stop.

If you want to be happy all day, count
your blessings. Be grateful!

Be positive! Anxiety destroys the joy of daily living.

No one is perfect. But we can perfect our nature if we live
with high principles, good habits, and positive vibrations.

How do you stay healthy and happy? Move the mind to
wisdom and inspiration. Move the body to hard work.

A positive attitude gives us health and peace of mind.

High standards are the foundation of a happy life.

What is more valuable than money or jewels?
Our positive attitude, good health, and high
principles. Nobody can steal them!

If we can live with ourselves peacefully,
we can face any challenge in life.

If we are always in a giving mode, we are content
and happy. If we are always in an expecting
mode, we are dissatisfied and unhappy.

For an inspired soul, every moment is an opportunity.

The extraordinary person does not
need to follow the crowd.

To be in harmony with others, we must
be in harmony with ourselves.

Eat moderately, speak to the point, and never
try to get away with doing very little.

Be gracious, not grouchy.

Gratitude and humility are the fuels which
power our internal improvement.

When we make excuses, we are practicing self-deception.

A strong mind has patience, perseverance,
and stamina, but not stubbornness.

To the wise, humility and congeni-
ality are the greatest strengths.

Once you learn to know yourself, you
will learn to know everything.

A wise person is deep, encouraging, and helpful.

Celebrate life by cultivating a deep understanding of it.

Life is merely a series of events. Deal with them from
the point of view of a wise and mature human being.

We should be shaped by our inner conviction, not by life's events.

When we fill our mind with inspiring thoughts, there
will be no room for anxiety and depression.

To believe that nothing is impossible is
the most powerful force in healing.

A good quality life comes from being
deep, creative, and sincere.

It is only through self-discipline that we
can gain control over our life.

Maturity doesn't mean being perfect. It means growing wiser every day.

A deep mind is the greatest healing device.

Keeping your mind and body fit is a spiritual practice. Spiritual improvement can only be maintained with a fit mind and body.

A person who does not yield to negativity is godly.

We show our love through our deeds, not just through our words.

Flush away all negative thoughts with inspiration!

There's no freedom without responsibility. There's no prosperity without hard work. There's no good reputation without a good nature.

Time is on the side of those who put it to work for self-improvement.

A youthful attitude makes life heavenly.

Laziness is not a picnic. It's a curse.

Actions speak louder than words, and
simplicity speaks louder than pomposity.

Self-discipline is the first requirement for good health.

A wise person may change his decision, but
he never compromises his principles.

Be positive! Anxiety destroys the joy of daily living.

A good attitude makes a happy mind.

Self-esteem is the reward of self-discipline.

Inspiration multiplies when we give it away.

We must make cheerfulness our constant companion.

People who are always improving the situation find ways, not excuses.

There is no greater strength than enthusiasm.

To a wise person, every moment is a golden opportunity.

Life is as good as the energy we put out.

We are happy when we challenge
ourselves and inspire others.

The mind is just a vessel. We determine its contents.

As long as we are breathing, we should
be vibrant and inspiring.

We are rich when we live within our means.

Life is all about facing challenges
with courage and patience.

When we put effort behind our good intentions, we can change for the better.

Inspiration is not just a thought. Inspiration is a way of life.

Without self-discipline, there is no freedom.

There is joy when we put out good energy
for ourselves and for others.

The greatest love is to be the best example for others.

To embrace challenges with a positive attitude is heaven.

Having a good attitude is as important as breathing.

Make yesterday's mistake today's lesson, not a problem.

Don't wait for good luck to happen to you. By
that time all the stars will have fallen.

No one is perfect, but no one has to
remain in their imperfections.

Bad attitudes make us remorseful. Good
attitudes make us resourceful.

Worry is a waste of time. It takes us away from inspiration.

If we take care of little things right away, then
we won't have a big problem later on.

A good mental attitude is very important.
Never have self-defeating self-talk.

He is a true achiever who gains peace
and success at the same time.

Take care of your health. Letting your health go down
the drain leads to a lot of complications in life.

Use time efficiently. Don't putter around like a scatterbrain.

Do important things right away. Don't let things slide.
Then you won't have a million things on your mind.

Postpone non-essentials. Eventually, you'll
find that you don't need them anyway.

Don't have strong images, preferences, and
demands. Be resourceful. Make the best of what
you have, instead of running out for things.

Count your blessings instead of your feelings and imaginary misfortunes.

Drop grudges. Don't live in the past. Don't dig up dead people and dead issues in your mind.

Be driven by inner inspiration rather than outer stimulation.

Be guided by wisdom rather than analytical or subjective thinking.

Encourage, help, and flow. That should be our motto.

Our mind is a reservoir of creativity when we apply wisdom.

To conquer ego, practice compassion, humility, and wisdom.

We should be hard working, but never lose our balance.

Always work with what you have and make it better.

Never miss an opportunity to inspire yourself and others in any situation.

All the blessings which are given to us are
lost if we take them for granted.

Every moment is an opportunity for an inspired person.

Putting out good energy creates happiness
for those around us and for ourselves.

To be happy, count your blessings, not your complaints.

Keep these three things in your heart:
– Compassion;
– Forgiveness;
– Humility.

Our good nature is a song of the heart.

Out of inspiration will be born solutions to all problems.

True compassion is limitless.

Every moment, every thought and every action counts.

www.ingramcontent.com/pod-product-compliance
Lightning Source LLC
Chambersburg PA
CBHW062022040426
42447CB00010B/2104
* 9 7 8 0 9 7 2 7 1 8 5 3 0 *